Family

My Daughter

There are times my Darling,
That I feel so lost in this world,
Because of the sadness I endure
Of a daughter that I love so much.

To see her suffer in pain,
Her emotional draws that make me so full of tears,
Should I be negative with God,
Should I ask him why?
A Loving and gentle girl,
This Soul of mine,
Is losing the strength she has in her?

What should I do,
What should I say?
If only I could make it all go away.
You have come to me
As an Angle from God,
So, you see why I am so confused and sad.
I should be thankful and that I am.
But to witness the sufferings of an amazing girl,
This girl of mine
That I Love so much,
I tear at a negative thought,
But I hope that this gracious God,
This Loving and forgiving God,
Will create a miracle,
For this girl of mine.

Katarina

I love her for who she is
With three children now
And a Partner
Who is her
Strength and loves her.

They are a quiet family
Not into
Fame and glory
But culture
And living life is their goal.

I pray for them
As a family
And love
Everything about them.

To my grandchildren

When the day is done
And my life
Comes to an end
Don't cry for me
My little ones
For I will always be
Around you
Watching and helping you
Along your way
Your Mum and Dad too
I will never leave you all.

As you grow up
Remember to whisper
To me your love
And always talk to me
And the voice you hear
Will be mine
Guiding you through life.

Grand Children

There are six in the clan
Five girls
One boy
And we wonder what their future is?

All that the parents can do
Is prepare them
For what the future holds.

As I watch their
Every move
Their responses
Their actions
I breathe a sigh of relief
For the guidance
By the parents
Are admirable
And I know that they are
In good hands.

I can leave this world
Knowing that my grandchildren
Will grow up
Good and decent children
Who will themselves
Pass the message
Of goodwill to their children.

Grand Children

I love this little girl called Olivia
I love this little boy called Sebastian.
They both have sisters whom they love so much,
They are all gifts of God to us
Whom we cherish and love.

I love the chatter and the laughter
I love the hugs and the kissers
And I love the secrets that they tell me about their weird
and wonderful fantasy friends.

They fill me with joy
They fill me with passion in life.

I love when they talk to the birds and the animals,
And their fright when Mr Spider comes along.

They hug me and tell me that they love me
It's worth every Cent to see them smile.

To see my kids prosper and be loved
And to see their kids secure in their parents arms,
Gives me joy for that's all I want.

My Daughter

I wish I could cry for this dear Angel of mine,
I Wish I could hug her and tell her that all will be fine!
For 20 years she has been suffering and still she makes it fine,
Her beauty, her laughter, her love and yet an amazing Smile.
You are an Angel and I love you so dearly,
Only Life can guide and wish you a path,
The times I have admired you for the roads you have taken "The Highs and the Low's"
And I know that there is greatness in what you have achieved and for that I am motivated and full of praise.
I cried for you, and I prayed for you and wish I could do more,
But here I am a simple soul that wishes a person so bright and so beautiful the best in Life.

My Son & Grandson

I watch the way they are connected
My son being the driver
Knowing that his son can do better.

I remember my life with my son
I never encouraged him nor
Was I there for him
I was travelling
My mind facing challenges
And completely
Not appreciating my Son
Who was determined from the age of 10 or so
To be a Volleyball player.

He has achieved his dreams
He was Captain of Irish International
Worked with some of the world's top
Sports people
Now involved in global sports
And I notice how my grandson
Looks up to him
Knowing that he has a
Cool Dad to steer him
All the way.

I am full of praise
To my Son and his wife
They are a Dream Team
That any child would love to have.

To a Lovely Human Being (My Brother)

As you get closer to another year
I reflect on you as a brother
Taking care of me
At home and at school.
I am eternally grateful
For the Scholarship you helped me get
To England
For the way you guided me
At the start of my Adult Hood.

I was never there for the challenges
You faced in your life
But you persevered
And always came out a winner.

Forgiveness
As always been your strength
A Smile as been your Love towards humanity.
No matter what you have achieved in Life
You are truly a disciple of Christ
Living a life and truly is of a Blessing.
My Loving Brother.

The Pillai Family (My son and family)

Thank you for the time we spent,
The beautiful home,
You have,
With the wonderful children you have.
Nicola!
You are the foundation that holds the family,
Nathan!
An amazing,
Husband,
Father,
And Son.
Life has taught you well,
The challenges you have overcome,
I admire you both,
For who you are.
Sebastian!
You are growing up,
And will make your parents proud.
Allegra and Valentina,
Be the amazing girls that you are.
My Love and hugs to you all

A Lovely Couple (My son & wife)

A couple who met when they were young,
Fifteen years later,
Married with three children,
And so much in Love.
They weathered the storms,
And have faced challenges,
Yet,
They grow stronger,
Each and every day.
I watch them hugging and kissing,
They cannot be separated for long.
Their children learn about Love,
From the examples that they witness,
They too are Loving.

This amazing couple,
Are my Son and Daughter-in-Law

My Grandchildren

I look at my grandchildren,
Their growth and maturity,
Is obvious.
Their Love,
So apparent,
Their energy to learn,
So obvious.
Their respect,
A credit,
To their parents.
I look at my grandchildren,
They carry with them,
The message,
Our parents taught us,
Love!

Lourdslin (my sister, my mother, my Friend)

A Lady of seventy and disabled,
Was in love with a wonderful man who too loved her till
his death.
She suffered to keep her family fed,
And travelled afar to be a Nanny,
Saved the money and bought the land to spilt between
her children.
They showed nothing but ingratitude,
They lacked the respect to this Lady of strength whose
only friend is God.
All she wanted was Love!
All she wanted was respect to the hardships she endured.
Instead, she endured abuse and insults.

God takes care of his flock,
Karma takes care of those who did wrong.
Angels live amongst us to serve Gods purpose,
Angels are those who rescued this Lady from abuse.

She will be amongst those who will Love her and tend to
her.
May God Bless You all.

A family of Perumal's! (My nephew and family)

Canny and Christine
A lovely couple
Who brought two children
Into this world.
A family
Who kept me sane
In this Sri Lankan
Life of gossip and vile rumours.
They laugh and joke with me
With no judgments
Or treacherous aims.
Wonderful offspring's
And well behaved.

Thank you
For your Love and laughter
Wishing you all
The Best

A lonely Lady (my Sister)

She sits all alone
With only the TV
To keep her company
And constantly awaits
To chat with me.
The sounds of vehicles
And people arguing
Makes her aware of life behind her walls.

She is a cultured and sophisticated
Lady
And yet
No one cares to sit and
Talk with her.
Her granddaughter
Comes now and then
But most of the time
It feels like a prison
Even though
Her son and family
Stay over but don't relate with her.

She is not one for
Sympathy and
Tears only flow privately.

She is strong
And positive
And yet
All alone.

Watching a Mass on TV
Is her only entertainment
I send her recipes
That excite her
But life
Is otherwise boring
And lonely.

My Sister who
Is still my Mother
And my best Friend.

My Son

I have watched the many times
You have had your highs and lows.
The many times that
Your Lover
Constantly gave strength to you
To be the man that you are.

She has been God sent
And as the Bible states
Nathan means a gift from God.
You two were meant for each other
Since you laid eyes on each other.

I watch the way
You work in sync with each other
The many challenges
You have faced together.

You are my Son,
I am proud of where you are
With a Loving wife
And Loving children.

I gave you nothing
But experience.
The Universe guided you
And I can only be proud of who you
Turned out to be.

A Strong Bond (My son & family)

I wish I had what they have
Face the challenges together
And not apart.
Nothing is easy in life
But together
They can move mountains
A hug and a smile
At the end.
Mature decisions
Not impulsive
Calculated moves
It's their Love
That helps them.
Children are a blessing
And their commitment
To the children
Are an example of their Love.
Be Strong
Together
You will navigate
The rough
And the smooth
Roads.
Be a family

Sebastian

☐Sebastian the venerable one
From Sebesta now Siva in Turkey.
Of his reverence
He is certainly a boy of
Compassion
Love
Thoughtfulness.
I watch the way his parents
Support him
The way his sisters tease him.
He is growing up
Following the guidance of his parents
Through the struggles and successes
They have experienced.

Sebastian a sweet and adorable boy
I love you as my grandson
As a wonderful human being
Who is part of changing the world
For the better.

My Daughter-in-Law

A strong and family Orientated Lady
Of Irish decent
Brought up to appreciate the values
Of Family
Trust
Togetherness
Love
And discipline.
My Son who in name is a gift from God
Has been gifted by beauty and strength
In his Wife.
She is fair
Understanding
But never cross her path
She is firm and her family comes first.
Through all that they have experienced
The hardships and the success they encounter
They remain grounded
She remains beautiful
And he remains secure
Knowing that she is his Rock.

Family

A family that stays together
Sticks together.
No scars of the past
Just beauty and laughter
As it should be.
We should embrace
This happiness
Their hard-earned success
Their Love for each other
The Love from their children
And let that Love prosper
As they grow up and mature.
All praise to the parents who hold it together

Grandchildren

All I want
Is to see them happy
Not influenced
By the past
Just being children
As they should be.

We have all faced hurdles
But the children
Should be protected
As much as possible
To help them grow.

So let's realise
That they are the
Only remaining ones
In our lives
Let's give them the best
For the future
Love them
And nurture
Them.

Grand Children

As you become parents and grandparents
You see yourself in life
As it evolves
In the form of children
Growing up
And being guided by experience
Hoping that they be a better version of us.
They are beautiful in our eyes
Well-mannered in our expectations
Nothing more we can do
But hope for the best
In their lives
Not knowing what their future holds
What their world will turn out to be.
They are sweet, adorable, Independent and confident
Thanks to their Parents.

Sebastian

I know a sweet little boy
Who has studied hard
To get into Grammar school.
He is a very thoughtful boy
A serious thinker.
He loves to cycle
Stops along the way
To look at insects
Frogs.
He stops along the Thames to watch the water flow
And sits and thinks.
He is kind
Loving
And I love him
Because he is my Grandson

The Adventures of the Five Scallywags

Book 1

Jungle Dream

By Quintus Pillai

Olivia, Sebastian, Esme, Allegra and Valentina are five young cousins who always played together whenever they meet. Olivia and Sebastian, the two oldest aged nine and eight are the leaders of the Scallywag gang. The rest being girls all aged 5, Esme and the twins Allegra and Valentina always followed the two oldest.

Olivia likes puzzles and is a girl with an enquiring mind. She likes to play the piano and other instruments whilst Sebastian likes maths and loves studying insects and lizards of all kinds. He loves playing rugby, fencing and karate.

Every time they get together, the Scallywags would decide on an adventure that will keep them away from their parents and any housework. Whilst on holiday in Sri Lanka, they decided to walk away from their holiday apartment near a well-known jungle which is famous for its vast collection of animals, birds, insects and snakes. The Scallywags were used to seeing wildlife on the TV in England and watch cartoons

about wildlife but have never experienced them in real life.
Aunty Brina had given them each a gift to take with them on holiday. Olivia was given a set of knitting needles to knit dolls clothes, Sebastian was given a toy hunting knife, Esme was given a stuffed leopard and the twin girls Allegra was given a family of stuffed monkeys and Valentina was given a toy of a jungle Tribal man.

Olivia and Sebastian are always protective of their little sisters. Olivia's sister is Esme and Sebastian's sisters are Allegra and Valentina. As they started their adventure, they all held hands and walked very carefully on the dried grass leaving footprints, listening to all the sounds of the birds. They tried to hear the monkeys or distant sounds of the elephants, but they did not hear any. Sebastian showed them the hunting knife he hid on the side of his trousers, there was a gasp of admiration for Sebastian, and everyone felt safe. Then Olivia took out a knitting needle that she had hidden under her dress and showed how she could prick an animal if it attacked them, and the rest went "Wow". The three little girls were a bit scarred saying that they want to return to their mummies, but Olivia has a commanding voice and calmed everyone down. As they walked, they could hear their own footsteps crushing on the grass and tried again to walk softly and making sure that they do not disturb an animal.

They walked past a bridge made of rope and under the bridge was an angry river with water gushing from the mountains and making thundering sounds. On the other side of the bridge was a tribal village and the chief was called Toto who has a thick moustache and beard. His job was to make sure that the tall grass was trimmed so that he can see any threats to the village.

The scallywags bent down and walked to make sure that they are not seen but Toto did not want them to know that he has seen them and was worried about the dangers in the jungle. A giant shriek of a sound from the peacocks caused the scallywags to hug each other, frightened and wishing that their parents were around.

But it's too late, they are in the jungle, and they are on their own. The sun was shining, and they were all thirsty. Olivia and Sebastian took off their rucksacks and gave each one a drink. Olivia left the bananas to the side, the sandwiches their mums had made and fruits onto a side. They were tired which made them sleepy. There were lots of sounds which they thought they knew. There was a slight breeze which made them all fall asleep under a dwarf coconut tree.

CHILDREN IN THE WOOD.

As they slept, a family of monkeys who have been watching the Scallywags ever since they entered the jungle, came down from the trees and walked slowly around them.

The young monkeys took the bananas but were soon stopped by the mummy monkey. She smiled at daddy monkey and looked again at the adorable children all fast asleep. Daddy monkey decided to climb a tall tree to see if there was any danger coming towards the children whilst mummy monkey collected leaves to cover the children from the heat. The scallywags were in dream land, and they were visited by all sorts of animals. The elephants were scary and blew their trumpets which caused the Scallywags to shudder. The leopards were angry and hungry and jumped on a spotted deer in front of the scallywags. Mummy monkey felt that the children were having a bad dream because of the screams they were making. Mummy monkey slowly caressed each of the children while the baby monkeys were eating the fruits and all the sandwiches. Mummy monkey was careful not to disturb the children. Daddy monkey came rushing down from the trees looking scared because he had seen a leopard coming towards where the children were asleep.

What are we to do said mummy monkey? Daddy monkey chased the baby monkeys up the tree whilst he and mummy monkey thought how to save the children. Mummy monkey knew of a bridge made of rope by the tribal people in the jungle to cross a terribly angry river. She also knew that the tribal people live close to the bridge and the leopard cannot cross that bridge. But there were five children, and they can only manage two, they had to think fast. Mummy monkey ran across the bridge to the tribal people jumping up and down and making sounds Ho ha ha-ha he and moving her arms. The tribal people heard her sounds but Toto the tribal leader made an angry growl that made the monkey move away. There were a group of young tribal children playing by the river who decided to investigate why the monkey was making the high-pitched sounds. They followed the monkey along the bridge always making sure that they don't look down as their parents have told them, but as the mummy monkey was looking back at the children she accidently fell in between the ropes and was hanging on the bridge. The screams from the children were heard by their parents who rushed towards the bridge.

The river was rough with the sounds of the crushing waves towards the rocks, the screaming children of the tribes and the parents rushing to rescue the monkey hanging on the bridge was exciting for Toto. Toto was brave and strong, and he helped pull the monkey up. All the tribal people, the children and the monkey were clapping their hands which made Toto enormously proud and happy.

It was at this same time that the parents of the Scallywags suddenly realised that there were no sounds from the children and being surrounded by the jungle suddenly caused them to be frightened and they too were screaming calling out their children's names. Daddy monkey heard the screams of mummy monkey, but he could not leave the children on their own, so he stood by the children hoping that mummy monkey will be OK. The baby monkeys were now screaming because they heard the screams of mummy monkey and by now the whole jungle was full of animal sounds because they knew that something was wrong.

The Elephants were sounding their trumpets, the snakes slowly moved underground, the birds flew in confused circles, the rabbits ran through the wild grass which frightened the deer who could not see what was moving the wild grass, they ran towards the leopard who was also confused with all the sounds in the forest and ran round in circles.

Meanwhile, the tribe people led by Toto followed the mummy monkey still wondering what the problem was.

While all the commotion was happening, the children were still fast asleep dreaming about Sebastian fighting with the big leopard and Olivia pricking the leopard with her knitting needle. Sebastian used his karate skills that he had learnt and his fencing skills together with his rugby skills to fight the leopard. Olivia used her piano skills to prick the leopard and her football skills to kick the leopard and the younger three scallywags were clapping encouragement to Olivia and Sebastian. The leopard was bleeding and getting tired while Olivia and Sebastian were getting more energy fighting the leopard.

The parents of the scallywags were following the crushed grass that the scallywags made to track the scallywags, they were frightened with tears in their eyes wondering if they will ever see their loving and beautiful children again. The night before, the parents were warned by a hunter that an angry leopard is nearby and to take every care with the children. They were desperately looking for the children.

Finally mummy monkey arrived making daddy monkey so happy to see her again but started to frighten the tribal people away to defend his family. Mummy monkey explained to daddy monkey that they could take the children to their parents in the tourist village. Daddy monkey helped the tribal people carry the children still in their sleep to the tribal village and rushed off to help mummy monkey take their baby monkeys to safety from the leopard. Meanwhile the parents of the scallywags heard the roar of the leopard nearby and decided to run back to their holiday home and call for help. As they entered their home, they were surprised to see all the scallywags fast asleep in their beds with crushed grass and dried leaves on them.

Olivia and Sebastian yawned and slowly opened their eyes and was so pleased to see their parents hugging them and crying. The three young scallywags woke up in excitement to the sounds of their parents and equally cried with happiness. None of the scallywags or the parents could understand how they got to bed until the hunter explained to them that he was with the tribal villagers who told him about a family of monkeys who helped save the children and the tribal people carried the children to their home. The next day together with the help of the hunter, the scallywag's families took bunches of bananas and fruits for the monkey family who were watching from high up in the trees, they came down as soon as the people left. The tribal villages too were given foods of various kinds by the parents of the scallywags. The stuffed leopard toy was strangely found in the jungle with its ears pulled and little holes all around its body. Only the scallywags knew that Sebastian's fighting skills and Olivia's knitting needle were used to fight the leopard. The whole tribal village, the tourist resort and the monkeys were confused when they found the toy leopard because they all heard a roar of the leopard.

That night, all the scallywags slept with their parents hugging them tight to make sure that their beautiful children are safe asleep.

The Scallywags want you to tell your parents where you are going because they love you and wish you to have a happy adventure.

The Adventures of the Five Scallywags

Book 2

The Jungle Safari

by Quintus Pillai

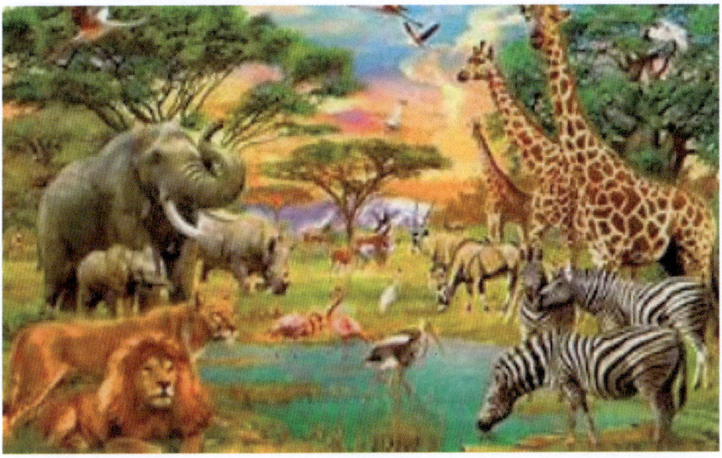

With the help of the Tribal Leader Toto, the parents of the five Scallywags decided to take them on a safari in the jungle. The scallywags were excited because they get to see all the animals also safely with their parents. Esme, Allegra and Valentina were happy that they can hold their mum's hand while watching the animals.

Toto was incredibly happy to lead the family into the jungle because this was his chance to show what a good Safari guide, he is. He went into the jungle and found his elephant mascot he uses for Safari tours and got four big elephants plus five baby elephants for the scallywags.

He also asked his wife Mama An to join him because she can cook the lunch for all of them. Mama An does not like elephants, so Toto got a tamed Ostrich and tied a harness on it. Mama An got on the bird to the laughter of the scallywags.

Esme, Allegra, and Valentina could not stop laughing, Olivia and Sebastian were trying to show respect but started laughing when the ostrich started going around and round to stop Mama An get on. Mama An did not like the laughter but also started laughing.

The scallywags laughed again when they saw their parents trying to get on the elephants, the elephants too were having fun with the parents by getting down and up while the parents were trying to get on. Everyone laughed when it was the scallywags turn to get on the baby elephants because the baby elephants have never had anyone on their backs. Allegra and Valentina were in tears while Olivia kept Esme calm by showing her how easy it was stroking the baby elephant. Finally, everyone was ready to go but the ostrich was not having it, it started making noises and tried to spread its wings making Mama A truly angry, one loud roar from Toto stopped the ostrich and it too was ready for the journey. Mama An is always proud of Toto because he takes care of her and the village tribe. He is an important man in the jungle too because the animals respect him as well.

Starting their journey into the jungle meant that they had to go through big tree bushes, looking out for snakes on the trees and cross deep lakes and rivers. Various insects and mosquitos too are a problem, so the scallywags were properly covered from top to bottom with mosquito nets, waterproof clothing, whistles to blow if they fell from the elephants and drink bottles round their necks when they are thirsty. They also had a cap to protect them from the heat of the sun.

As they set off, Toto led the way making sounds that only the elephants knew what it meant. Toto kept cutting leaves as he made a path, his spear always ready to use if a leopard attacked. Everyone felt safe with Toto leading the way. The mums were behind the children making sure that they do not lose sight of them. As they moved through the jungle, the monkeys were tickling the scallywags by using their tails to hang on the trees.

There was laughter from the scallywags, but Olivia's mum remembered a monkey peeing on her when she was young and was protective of her children.

A woodpecker making a hole in a tree flew past them and they all looked to see where it landed, a large eagle carrying a fish was spotted by Esme and she shouted to everyone to

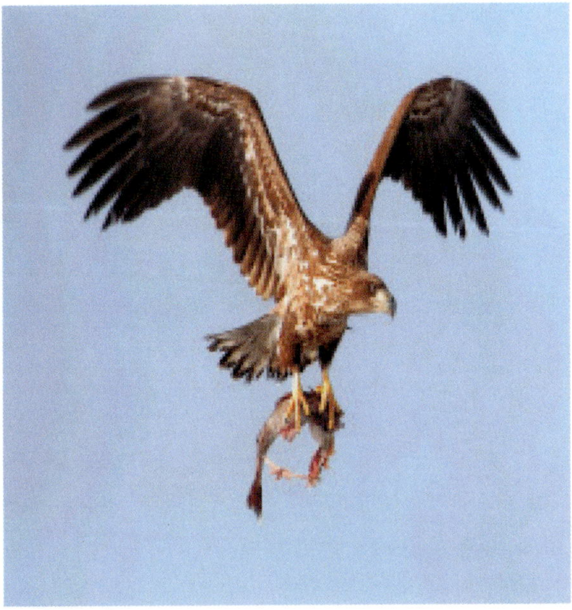

look. Allegra saw a snake on the ground and screamed. Valentina saw a spotted deer run across the jungle while Olivia and Sebastian were stroking their baby elephants to be calm and gently spoke to them. The scallywags were feeling proud that they are in the jungle and can't wait to go back and tell their friends of their adventure. As Toto was leading the group, they came across a river where Toto decided to stop and dismount. He commanded the rest of the elephants to get down and helped the scallywags to get down from the baby elephants. "This was a good place to rest and have lunch" he said to Mama An.

The parents decided to swim and bathe by the river while Toto took his spear and dived down deep into the river looking for good fish for lunch. Olivia and Sebastian decided to snorkel so that they can see Toto fishing and see the fish. The big black crabs by the river edge had their claws up in case the scallywags tried to come near them. Mama A held Esme, Allegra and Valentina and was careful in taking them into the jungle. She showed them the herbs and spices to break while she tore the banana leaves to use as plates and she plucked some mango, papaya and pineapples. Esme saw some Corn on the cobs and all three broke them from the plants. Mama A started to make a fire and as soon as Toto came out of the river. He had eleven fish for each of them. As Olivia and Sebastian came from the river, they saw Esme, Allegra and Valentina chase butterflies and joined them but soon it was time for lunch because the smells of herbs burning on the fish made them hungry. The fish were laid on the banana leaves with the corn on the cob and everyone used their fingers to eat. The food was very tasty. After lunch, Toto and Mama An, put all the banana leaves into the fire because they respect the jungle and make sure that it is always left clean. While the parents rested, the scallywags visited a cave always making sure that they can see their parents. Toto and Mama An also watched the children. Olivia said that there might be a Dinosaur in the cave, Sebastian thought that a large Monitor Lizard could be living in the cave. The twin girls thought that there were Unicorns whilst Esme thought that Peppa Pig was in the cave. Suddenly, there was a big roar from the cave and the scallywags ran towards their parents. Mama A suddenly rushed into the cave and brought two tribal children from the cave who always frighten tourists' children with sounds with seashells.

The scallywags were pleased to meet the children and played games with them and had a lot of fun. Meanwhile, Toto made a small spear for Sebastian and a necklace with a leopard's tooth for Olivia. Mama An made necklaces for the three smaller scallywags.

It was time to mount the elephants and Toto had a surprise for the group. Mama A decided to release the ostrich to the jungle and Toto helped her ride with him on his elephant. The scallywags waved the tribal children goodbye. As they moved through the jungle, there was a sudden opening, a large waterfall can be seen with more tribal children bathing under the waterfall. On the far side there a stream where all the animals and birds, elephants, leopards, deer, rabbits, foxes, wolves, flamingo's, cattle, buffalos, and all other animals were all drinking together.

Strangely, one of the leopards had a knitting needle on its back and Olivia and Sebastian looked at each other. Toto too noticed it and looked back at Olivia and Sebastian. The scallywags were so pleased to have visited the jungle and it was time to return to the holiday resort. Toto led them to an area where there was a Safari Jeep waiting to take the family. Toto gifted Olivia and Sebastian their gifts. Mama A had tears in her eyes when putting the necklaces on the three little scallywags. It was so sad to see Toto and Mama And go into the jungle on the elephant while the rest of the elephants and baby elephants
were released into the jungle.

It was time to pack up and go to the airport for the Scallywags to fly back to England. They could not wait to go home and tell their friends of their adventures.

Adventures of the Super Quins during lockdown

By Quintus Pillai

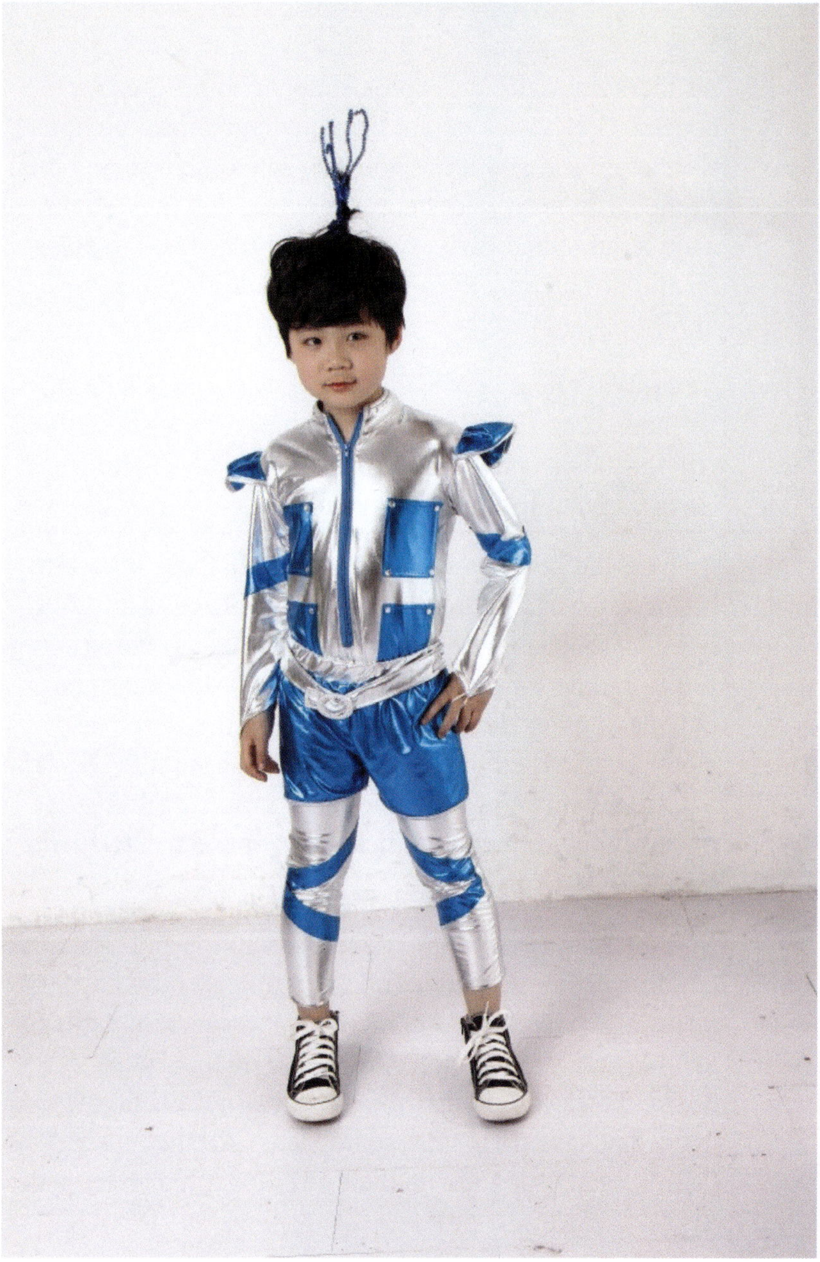

As the Virus caused people to stay at home, the five cousins Olivia, Sebastian, Esme, Allegra and Valentina were confused about not going to school, not seeing their friends. But they were happy knowing that they do not need to go to bed early, wakeup early, no need to dress up and no screams from their parents asking them to hurry up.

In the Wakefield house, Olivia is always the leader in her house and Esme always looks up to her sister Olivia. Olivia is always thinking positive, and she is strong and leads Esme to listen to Mum and Dad.

In the Pillai house, Sebastian is sad! He loves his sports; he loves when Dad talks to him about Rugby and Football. Sebastian loves everything that has do with sports and he is proud of his dad. Sadly, he cannot go outside to play. He is stuck at home with his two sisters who scream when they want something and like Olivia, Sebastian knows how to stop them from screaming. He makes fun with them and tickles them and makes them laugh.

Both parents are trying to keep a discipline and make the children do some schoolwork, they realise how much of respect they have for the schoolteachers in being able to keep the children to concentrate and do their work. At home, the children think it's a holiday but it's not. It's important says their Mums and Dads! All the Super Quin's can think about is their next adventure. This will help them forget the boring time at home, the food and watching television with news about the Virus, Virus and Virus. This is boring said Olivia, Esme repeats what Olivia has said, and Mum tries to explain the problem. But it's boring Mum, can we not go to the park and play with our friends? I miss them, Mum. Esme too has tears in her eyes but let's Olivia talk. Olivia goes with Esme to their bedroom and shuts the door. Poor Mum hugs Dad because she is feeling so sad for the children and is exhausted with trying to find things for them to do.

In the Pillai household, Mum is not having any of the complaints, Sebastian knows that it's important not to upset Mum. Also, Dad is around, so he whispers to Allegra and Valentina to also go to their bedrooms.

The Super Quin's decided to call each other to think about what they should do, the thought of playing games, create some other things to do, it was getting boring. Esme had a bright idea, why don't we go to sleep and dream about an adventure? Allegra and Valentina jumped up and down excited about a new adventure. Olivia wanted everyone to be calm because they do not want the parents to know. She said to Sebastian to allow the girls to sleep in bed with him and Olivia asked Esme to get into her bed, Esme had to climb the bunkbed to hug Olivia. Olivia was on the phone to Sebastian. What is the adventure Sebastian, asks Olivia? What about the Safari? We have done that says Olivia. What about School? Esme says, Olivia and Sebastian both say, "That's Boring" and everyone laughs. Allegra and

Valentina look at each other, their minds thinking, and they both shout out "why don't we fight the Virus?". Great idea shouts Olivia, Esme and Sebastian both shout out" what is the Virus?". Olivia explains, its invisible, we cannot see it, but it is dangerous, and we must fight it to save the world. People are dying from it, young and old. We are losing so many people and it is so sad. Our Grandparents too are sad because they cannot visit us and are worried about the virus because they are old and can easily get it.

Sebastian said, "We must make the virus look like something, because if its invisible, we cannot fight it", good idea says Olivia. Olivia asked everyone to close their eyes and think of what the Big, Bad, Ugly Virus should look like? This so difficult shouts Allegra What about Grandpa being the Virus shouts Sebastian and they all laughed. Olivia shouts at everyone to think again and suddenly Olivia had an idea "what if we think of an animal that we are scared of, we can make that be the Virus?". Esme shouted "Snakes", but Olivia loves snakes. Valentina shouted "Insects", but Sebastian loves insects. What about an Elephant shouted Allegra? That is too big said Olivia. Olivia saw a rubber orange ball in the corner of her room with spikes and she was so excited and put the mobile phone on FaceTime for Sebastian, Allegra and Valentina to see what she thinks the Virus should be. Sebastian too had an orange ball with spikes. They all agreed, they had something they could now dream about and see how the Super Quin's were going to change the world. Sebastian asked, "What does a virus do?", Olivia said "that's a good question", Esme said "Why don't we ask Mum and Dad? They all ran to their Mums and Dads and excitedly asked what a virus was? The Wakefield's explained that when people get the Virus, they breathe it in, they cannot breathe, it makes them ill and some of them die. That is why we must wear face masks, gloves, aprons and we must wash our hands. The Pillai's explained that Dad has Asthma, and it is dangerous for Dad to get the Virus, so we must try and protect Dad. Both parents explained why it is important to stay at home and not mix with people, hug people, shake hands with people not even your grandparents. This was sad for the Super Quin's; they cried and hugged their parents. They told them how much they loved them and said that they will be good children. Poor Esme, Olivia had to hug her and take her back to the bedroom. Allegra and Valentina too were held by Sebastian and taken to the bedroom. All the Super Quin's wished they were together because they wanted to hug each other but they cannot because of the nasty Virus.

Olivia is always the leader of the Super Quin's and she wanted everyone to be strong and to think, she wiped her tears, but she knew she had to be strong for the rest of the Group. Sebastian was also whipping tears and did not want his sisters to see him like that. Their Mums and Dads came into their rooms and allowed Esme to sleep with Olivia and for Allegra and Valentina to sleep with

Sebastian. It was late at night, and they had to go to sleep. The Super Quin's hugged the orange ball with spikes and slowly went to sleep.

As then went deep into their sleep, they met in a room that is special for the Super Quin's. They were all standing in a circle and behind each of them was a big tube with the front opened. Has they moved back into the tube, the machine started working, a Silver Suit was fitted to them with solar panels on their backs. This was to help the sun rays to energise the Power Jets that will be fitted on them. They were fitted with goggles with infrared glasses so that they can see at night and the viruses. A laser beam was fitted on the goggles connected with a button fitted to their right hand. The laser beam is to destroy the viruses. A jet engine with a booster was fitted at the back of their costume to help them fly and the button was fixed to their left hand. They were also fitted with an Earpiece connected to a Radio transmitter which helps them talk to each other. This is amazing said Sebastian who loves being a Superhero. Olivia was thinking as to how to get the team of Super Quin's work together. After the fittings were completed, they all gathered round in the centre of the room with Olivia in the centre. She told them that it was their duty to save their Mums and Dads, their Aunties and Grandparents, their cousins and their friends and in fact the whole wide world.

They hugged each other and followed Olivia outside. While she was deciding on how to kill all the viruses,

Sebastian pressed the jet booster button on his left hand which made him fly up and up into the sky. He just did not take his finger off the button. He flew through clouds and was amazed to pass birds, planes and as he was looking down, he could see the houses getting smaller and smaller. Suddenly he was up in Space, and he could see the Earth and was surprised to see all the viruses surrounding the world. The orange balls with spikes were so close with each other that he could hardly see the green grass or the waters in the ocean. He was so excited he called the rest of the Super Quin's to fly up at once. He was screaming with excitement, and he could hardly hold his breath. Olivia told him to calm down on the radio has the rest of the Super Quin's raised up and up in the air. Poor Allegra nearly hit a bird, but she was all right. The Super Quin's felt they have the power, and has they raised towards Sebastian who was in Space controlling his jet booster to remain stationary, he was pointing his finger down to earth. They all looked down and could not believe what they saw. Olivia decided that they all form a circle facing outward and point their laser beams to earth. Olivia said that on the count of three that they all press their laser buttons. One, two, three and suddenly the whole earth was ablaze with viruses being destroyed by the laser beams. The Super Quin's were shouting "Take that naughty virus", "we do not want you killing the people we love". They were so excited that back in the house, their parents woke up wondering why the children were shouting in their sleep. The parents were hugging them, but the children were so strong and pushed the parents aside. Esme, Allegra and Valentina were screaming in excitement, Sebastian was shouting "Shoot them, shoot all of them" and Olivia was guiding them to stop, and, in her sleep, she was shouting "Stop". The parents were laughing knowing that the Super Quin's were on some exciting mission, but they did not know what. Back in space, all was quiet after the viruses were destroyed but Olivia knew that there was still more work to do. She used to list to mum and dad talk about the hips in the ocean with people stuck and dying due to the virus, so she asked everyone to follow her. They sped down to earth and Olivia was taking them to the ocean looking for ships of all sorts. She spotted the Queen Elizabeth Ship, and she can see viruses all-round the ship and with their infrared goggles they can see the viruses inside the ship as well. On Olivia's command, they pressed their laser beams and burnt the viruses and sped off to clear all the ships on the ocean from the virus. The sun rays were powering the jet boosters and the morning sun was beginning to rise. Sebastián said that he wants to fly home to kill any viruses around Mum and Dad, Allegra and Valentina followed him. Olivia and Esme decided to do the same with their Mum and Dad and frightened the cats in the Wakefield house, because animals can see invisible things. Mum and Dad were hugging each other fast asleep in both houses.

Olivia called on the radio asking everyone to meet at Aunty Brina's house to make sure that she is safe. The Super Quin's have a special place in their hearts for

Aunty Brina because she buys them expensive gifts, allows them to stay at her place but she is extremely strict with them. They love her dog, Willow and her cat, Duchess. As they flew into the house, Duchess and Willow got the shock of their lives and started make noises. It was incredibly early in the morning and Aunty Brina needed her sleep. She woke up due to the noise and the Super Quin's were huddled together in the front of her bed. She was staring right at them, but they were not sure if she could see them. Aunty Bina is a Super Woman because every day she must fight the pains in her body. She is amazing and does not complain or cry. Willow the big Hungarian Wisler got into the bed and put her head on Sabrina's lap making her go back to sleep. The Super Quin's quietly left the house, but Esme could not help but make Duchess jump with fright, Olivia shouted at Esme, but Esme was laughing and so was Allegra and Valentina. The Super Quins decided to go to their teacher's homes and their friend's home to clear any viruses before they head back to bed. Finally, they decided to visit an old gentleman, Captain Tom who himself is a world hero for helping the NHS and inspiring people and communities worldwide for his work to help raise £30M. Like the Spitfire and Hurricane fighter planes that flew past his home, the Super Quin's did a Fly Past his home whilst he was asleep and made sure that no viruses were around him. He is a special man, and he deserved their respect like all children round the world gave respect to him. This has been an amazing journey for the Super Quin's. They saved the world from the virus, but nobody will know that it is the Super Quin's that saved the world. Suddenly it was morning and has Olivia woke up she looked for Esme, yes! Esme must be in bed with Mum and Dad. At the Pillai's household, the story was the same, Sebastian woke up only to find that Allegra and Valentina were both snuggled up in bed with Mum and Dad.

Suddenly, there was a known on the door of the Pillai and Wakefield homes. Their Mums as usual went to see who it was? It was the Postman with packages for the Super Quin's. The Super Quins excitedly open their gifts, and they were shocked to see the Silver Costumes with Solar panels on the back, Goggles with infrared glasses, a Laser beam and a Jet fitted in the back of the costume. A little card fell off each of their boxes. It read "To the amazing Super Quin's from Duchess, Willow and Aunty Brina" They were shocked, and they all got on FaceTime to thank Aunty Brina, but sadly even Super Woman needs her beauty sleep!

Early Morning, their Mums and Dads were in front of their TV's, the religious people were saying how they saved the world from the virus, politicians were saying that they were responsible and some silly man in America was saying that he helped clear the virus with disinfectant. Crazy!

The Super Quin's want all children, Mums and Dads and grandparents to know that you are all heroes.

Those who made an impact in my Life
Apart from Family

Her Majesty! The Queen

I was visibly moved
By the graciousness
Of our Queen.
Even during her own sadness
She stood in silence
With a tear flowing
Standing on behalf of a Nation.

You dare not talk
About the strength
Of a woman
For she was all that and more.
Families may be divided
But as the Matriarch
She stands firm
And tall
Amidst the sadness
Around the world.

She has weathered
Many storms
Weathered insults
Yet
She stands
In silence
Has her Right Arm is slowly
Lowered to rest.

May God strengthen our gracious Queen.
The Nation

The World
Want you to rest
To gather your thoughts
Of the amazing Love
And Life you led
With your consort.

Don't Cry for me Sri Lanka

Don't cry for me Sri Lanka
We have been battered
And denied our rights
As citizens of a great land called
Sri Lanka.

Don't cry for me Sri Lanka
The worst is almost over
For we the people
Are making the change
And we the people will make
Sri Lanka Great Again.

Cry for Freedom
Cry for being
One people
One Nation
Cry for Justice

Don't pity us
We have weathered the storms
And we are strong
Sri Lanka
We cry for Peace.

Mike Calton ex British Royal Marines

I know that he volunteered
To serve his country.
I know that he was proud
To be of service.
The compensations he received
For what he suffered
Is far less
Than a Refugee will be awarded
For what they have suffered.

It's not fair
To convince young people
To go to war
Without telling them
Of the lack of support
They will receive when they return.

He is a compassionate guy
A true mark
Of a disciplined soldier
Always at your side
If you need help
And yet
I cannot comprehend
What he goes through
How lonely he must feel
And still
A Patriot no matter what.

I am pleased
That he has an Angel with him
Who supports him
And loves him
No matter what.

Nigel Goldsack (London-based producer Nigel Goldsack, whose credits include *The Merchant Of Venice* and *The World Is Not Enough*, died suddenly aged 62 on October 2018.)

I met this man in 2019
A beautiful man
Whose presence
Made me want to spend
As much time as possible.

He was a very sincere man
And I am certain
That everyone he met
Warmed up to him.

He used to tell me
About his wife's
Holiday in the Lake District
And he took a keen interest on me.

I wished
I told him
How I felt
About his presence.

He truly was a wonderful
Human Being
Which is why
God needed his help.

Dino Baptiste (*Best Boogie Woogie and Blues Pianist*)

From the first day we met
I have been impressed
Of your contagious
Smile and laughter
Your charismatic aura
Your warm hugs
And your abundant energy.

The world may be in distress
But the time spent
Listening to your talent
Gives us that few minutes of escape
From the Rhythm & Blues.

Play on Dino
Your music is the drug
That I so desire.

A lonely man (Alex, a gifted artist)

I know a man,
A very lonely man,
With little contact with his family,
Lives on his own.

I know a man,
I love his soul,
He is a gifted artist,
He is not to be blamed for his addiction,
I know this man.
We are not to judge,
But help,
We may have our own demons,
Yet, we are not to judge,
At a time of crisis,
We show ourselves,
Our compassion or selfishness,
Money can't buy love,
It's love, true love that matters.
I know this man,
A true spirit of a being,
His love is far away,
He is trustworthy,
He is loyal,
He is not at fault,
I will forever be at his side.

True Beings with Love (Alexander, Stoke on Trent)

Never judge people
Who have physical and mental issues.
They are sent to test us
With Love.
If you spend time with them
You will know
That all they want
Is to give Love and receive Love.
They are beams of Love
And we need to receive them
Accordingly.

Love is the one thing
That heals us
Make us smile
Make us happy
Make us energised.
Absorb this
From those sent to help us.
They are special beings
On Earth.

Ingrid Gere (Amsterdam, Netherlands Died: 7th June 2012. I travelled overnight to visit her before she died. She raised her hand and stroked my face and that was all the energy she had. My poem was read at her funeral)

In the deepest and darkest moments of your life,
You are still strong as a rock.

Even with pain around you,
You steer to take control and as a warrior,
You never give up.

I do not know much about you Ingrid,
But I wish to know all aspects of your life.

I have never related to your life,
But I want to be there for you.

I cannot force my wants,
But bow to your every request.

I just want to Hug you and take away the pain.
I want to see you and even shed a tear,
This amazing woman, so strong and yet so in need.
I want to be there and kiss you as you sleep,
I want to do all but at this moment of time,
I just want to be there!

The only manager who believed in me (British, when I worked at Philips Telecoms, Dublin, Ireland)

I ponder ,
Of the days we worked together,
The relaxed ways,
You ran the office,
The respect you showed to others,
The support you gave to me.
Jackie too was a part of that life,
The way she brought me down to Earth,
By showing that life was more important,
Than my success at work.
You are both a treasure in my Life,
And now with the news of your cancer,
It just shows how valuable you have been in my Life.
How grateful I am,
In meeting such an amazing couple.
Thank you both for your Love and Friendship.
We will meet soon,
That my friends is a promise.

Giovani Isola (My customer from Como, Italy died in 2012. An amazing and loving gentleman)

A fine jolly Italian from Como,
I knew him so well and always longed to meet him.
He would put his arms around me and walk me through the streets of Como,
with his son beside him,
Interpreting each word he said to me.

He sadly died in 2012,
I did not have the funds to be at his side,
But I shed so many tears since I loved this jolly old gentleman from Como.

I think of him through these sad times,
He raises my spirits,
He makes me smile,
We need more people,
Like Giovani Isola,
From Como, Italy,
A wonderful, generous, loving, husband, father and a dear friend of mine.

Teresa (she was my Customer Services Manageress in Ireland up to 1996. I finally tracked her, and we stay friends)

Where do you go to
When you are alone?
Where does your mind travel to
When you wish to hide your pain?
You walk in the forests
Through scenic routes
Stopping now and then
To shed a tear
Creating a pool of sadness
Reflecting a life
That can be full of joy
If only you had Love
Which you so desire
At this very moment.

So, where do you go to
When you are alone and sad?
I wish I can hug you
And say that it's alright
Make you smile
Make you laugh

Images *(Hildegard Breuer, German. I met her in 1973, we lost contact in 1979, in 2009 whilst I was living in Dubai, she tracked me via Face Book. We have since stayed in contact.)*

Three images
All so similar
Reflecting a picture
That surrounds my thoughts.

I cowardly turn away
For the feelings inside me
Long to reach out and touch
Not the image but the picture
Far, far away
But feelings are hard to bear
And the images become the picture.

Three pictures
All so similar
Reflecting an image
The likeness of you.

Two Shining Stars (Ieva Strupule, Latvian, a successful CEO in Oslo, Norway. Recognised as a Global Shaper by the World Economic Forum)

We are two stars
That collided
One guiding the other
Through the
Twists and turns
In life.

Always look
For the beacon of light
For it is I
Your star
Guiding you
Through life
Always around you
Always at your side.

I think of you
As I walk through
Life
And always
Picture your beauty
And your smile.

My English Rose (A Lady throughout)

I finally found my English Rose,
An elegant Lady of upper class,
With a passion for the good things in life.
I love to watch you move to music,
Watch your beauty in a feminine way,
Love to hear your voice as you express a love of the opera,
You bring true meaning to beauty.
I wish I can hold you, hug you, and whisper sweet things in your ears.
Love has no boundaries,
Love has no age,
Love has no limits,
What Love has is an abundance of a need to say, "I Love You" and watch the most beautiful Smile from the one you love.

Walk of Love (Danish, she inspired me in Love)

As I walked through the forest this morn,'
You were with me in Spirit.
I held your hand,
And every step we took,
It was a step of Love,
Every movement of your body,
Blended with the movement of the forest,
And every breath you took,
Was a gentle breeze?
And I breathed the "Breath of Love."
And as we ended our "Walk of Love"
I could not release the Spirit in you,
And hoped that like the Sleeping Beauty,
You awoke with a dream on your mind.

Our one-year anniversary (My Partner 19/07/2021 to 01/08/2022)

I waited for her as the train pulled into the station
Although the crowd exited the train
I saw her clearly
Her hair flowing to the wind
As I admired her beauty
And was attracted by her smile.

As she sat on the balcony
Sipping herbal tea
I was thankful
For her being in my life.

That evening has she relaxed
I was excited to cook
Our celebration dinner
Italian chilli prawn linguine.
The aroma filled the room
And she expressed how hungry she was.

As we sat to celebrate our
One year anniversary
We raised our glass of wine
Looked at each other and sipped the wine.
Her beauty still glowing
As she put a spoonful of
Italian chilli prawn linguine
In her mouth
Her face exploded
And yet she composed herself

And I regretting
The amount of chilli flakes
I added.

She was in pain
Her lips numb
The taste buds were gone
She clearly was not enjoying the meal
And I
Regretting what I did.

It was a night to remember
But
For all the wrong reasons
On our One Year Anniversary.

The New Forest

I knew him since 1972
He became my Best Friend.
We travelled and stayed at Youth Hostels
Those memories
Are one that impacted my life.

Our friendship ended
Like a thunderbolt
And that impacted my life too.

The many friends
I thought I had in this tiny village called
Brockenhurst
A place I made a home
For one year or more.

The many adventures I had
The funny things
We experienced
And the many barbecues we had
They are memories I hold so dearly
In my heart.
And the one who made it all possible
Was a lady from Bremen
Who is so dear in my heart.

Cristina Cabrejas

She has a beauty that I am
Attracted to
But she would prefer
Her beauty inside
More than her outside.

She is passionate
About peace
And her love
Is her work
And sacrifices
Romance to her passion.

I long to hear her voice
To remind me of the
Tango
We once danced.

She never talks about
Hardship
Her issues
Just a constant list of
Projects
She creates and recognised
By VIPs round the world.

She is a nomad
And blends with all cultures
And a citizen of
The world.

I pray for her
Because she needs to be recognised
For her creative contributions
For World Peace.

Environment

COVID-19

The Assassin has finally got its victim,
An old man,
Selfish and careless,
About the people and the country,
He represented,
The world he should have protected.
The world poured scorn,
On this decrepit old man,
Now Karma,
Has finally said,
Enough is enough!

We don't wish you well,
Mr President!
We hope that the USA,
The world,
Will forget this evil clown,
And move forward,
In uniting together,
To be in Peace with each other.
COVID-19,
Has finally got its victim

WHERE DID WE GO WRONG!

☐I dream of a hug
A kiss
A dance
A gathering!
Where did we go wrong?

I miss my Partner,
My children,
My grandchildren,
My family in Sri Lanka
Where did we wrong?

I miss my friends
The walks to Borough Market,
The occasional dance at a club
The London scene
The beautiful parks
The mountains
The canals
Where did we go wrong?

It is so lonely
Watching TV
Listening to music
Cooking for me
The news about Covid
And this irritating Trump
Where did we go wrong with our choices?

The Environment

The air is cleaner,
Fewer planes in the skies
Fewer news of atrocities,
The Ozone Layer
Is reducing in size
The conglomerates are being controlled
We crave for love
We think of family
The animal kingdom is more at ease
Less materialism
Less greed
More hygiene
More care
More Love
Mother Nature is teaching us
Let's Listen and Learn

A New Beginning!

When this is all over,
I wonder and ponder what the reactions will be?
Will we rush back to what was normal,
Will those of us who relished in the Peace and
Quietness,
Escape back to our comfort zones of the mountains,
forests, beaches to absorb our hunger for peace and
quietness?
I am enjoying this time of Self Awareness,
To understand the importance of simplicity in my life,
To rid of the toxics in my life,
To venture forward,
In strength,
No matter what changes are in store from Mother Earth.

The Virus

This virus has caused us to rethink!
It's exposed those who are selfish and vindictive,
It's made governments spend on their people,
It's made institutions back down,
It's made people the focal point.
The air is a better quality,
The animal world has breathed a sigh of relief.

People have started to care for each other,
Love has spread in an amazing way,
Even the religious are confused,
Their Godliness is questioned in many ways,
Because it's those who practice what they preach, survive!

The world will discard the evil,
Good will survive,
It will be a place we will not take for granted,
Only we can decide it's future!

Tragedy

With all this technology,
We are still at the mercy of Mother Earth!
All the wealth,
The weapons,
The fact that we have been to the moon,
We are still at the mercy of Mother Earth!

We have received so many warnings,
Many tragedies and famine,
Yet we never listened,
We were greedy,
We ignored the poor,
The lands of others,
We ventured to impress others of our way of life,
We created genocides,
Equality was " In Principle",
Rape was OK by the judge,
We thought we were God!

Today!
We are at the mercy of Mother Earth,
We depend on the low paid for help,
Have we learnt?
Do we accept our faults,
Are we sorry for the damage we have caused?
What about religion and their representation to God?
Have we learnt?
The time for healing is not over,

We have to bow down to Mother Earth,
While our loved ones leave this earth.
Have we learnt?
Only Mother Earth will know!

God is not at fault!

We are but human,
Full of faults and weaknesses,
Yet we believe that we have the right to judge others,
The right to instil our beliefs on others,
The right to change the way of life on others,
All in the name of their God, their Prophet, their
Saviour.

Yet, the destruction they leave behind,
Is beyond belief,
The sufferings they have caused,
The divisions they have created,
All in the name of God?

Whether it's a country or an individual,
I despise you as a human being,
For your acts which cannot be blamed on God,
But you as thoughtless human beings,
Who prey on the innocent,
Attack for materialist greed,
Or like the Pharisees showing ignorance of a pious pose.

The world is changing,
We have to rid our lives of this toxic waste,
To help us be calm and content with true souls that
express love in whatever way or form.

It will go away!

I know it's Covid
I know it's lonely
But don't let it get you down
Smile,
It will go away.

I know that it's lonely
On your own
This Christmas time
It's Covid I know
But don't let it get you down
It will go away.

Our Love
Will never fade away
Our Smile
Will never fade away
Our happiness
We can always create that
Don't let Covid rule us
It will go away

Book of Places

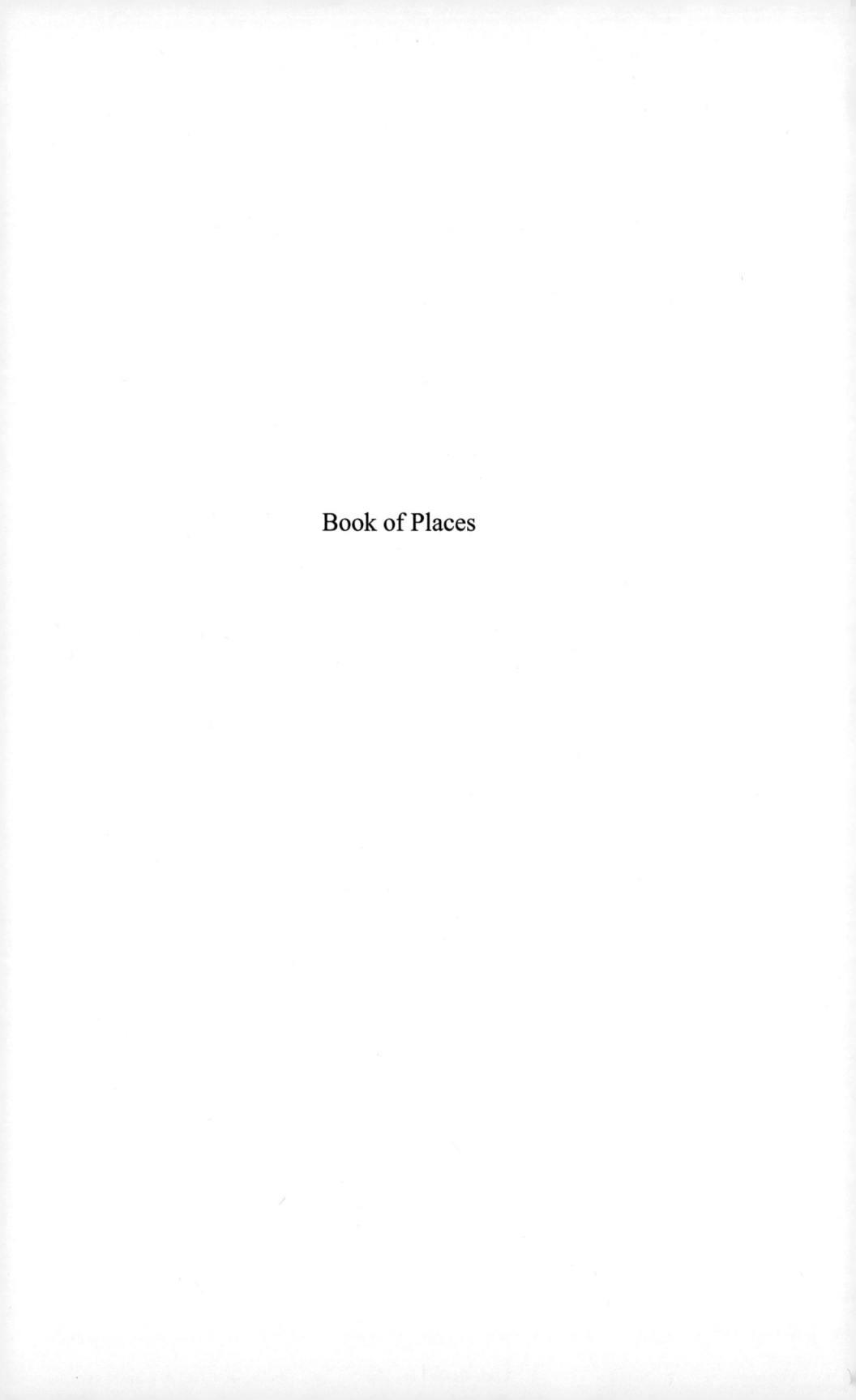

Winkle (Wangle Winkle – Reutter, Austria)

The snow-covered mountains
The snow-covered trees
The snow-covered village
A place I like to make my home.
The views are a dream
The sights of roaming deer
The colourful scenery
Summer or winter
The people so friendly and welcoming.
Twice have I been here
Twice have I seen
The warm greetings that never goes cold.
A home they can make for me
A family I am in
But the days pass so fast
That my home
I must leave.
How sad I feel
That every time I love
Beauty in all forms
It is the only time
That destroys my happiness.

The Fish (by the Blue Danube – Ness Dorf, Vienna: 30th July 1975)

I am a fish,
And I travel all day,
From one end of my home to the next,
Searching for food,
Behind plants and rocks and at times the riverbed itself.

I had so many friends,
But now they are few.
Yesterday I lost a friend,
And today, I lost another.
It is so strange,
Worms drop into our home,
My friend,
She said it tasted well,
But suddenly she disappeared,
I have not seen her anymore.

Today, it happened again,
But my friend did come back,
Her body was bloody,
And she was trying hard to swim,
But the currents carried her away.

I see another worm,
They are strange little worms,
I think I will just go away.

The Coastguard Cottage

A place from nowhere,
So serene and silent,
Except for the sound of the waves,
the sounds of excitement from the birds when the tide comes in.
We watched the sunrise from our bedroom,
While Minnie watched the rabbits on the wild seagrass.
It is a place of peace that allowed me to draft my book,
It allowed us to rekindle our Love.
We walked past the sheep as the cattle viewed us from the fields and looked at wild mushrooms that grew in the sand dunes at Goswick beach.
So grateful for the time and the long walks along the secluded beach,
holding hands with the one I Love.

The streets of London

I walked the streets of London,
As the sun rose to greet this once busy city,
But now a lonely deserted street,
Looking more like a ghostly town.

I admired old buildings that once were camouflaged by
the crowded streets of the hustle and bustle.
The distant sounds of ongoing construction,
Distracted this quiet city,
With no smells of diesel or leaded fumes,
The streets are empty of the Pinstriped men and women ,
Who would otherwise be rushing to make their next
million dollars,
Whilst the poor begged on the streets,
To feed their hunger.

I visited Borough Market,
A once busy market with all types of foods,
Cafes, restaurants and wine bars,
The emptiness is a reminder than a change is in the
horizon,
A distant echo of a sound from a fisherwoman fills the
halls of this quiet market,
The smells of the aroma from a cheese stall are inviting.

I walked back along the River Thames,
And over bridges that that once held the memories of
London's past,

Breathing the fresh air,
Warmth from the sun,
Admiring the beauty of this great cosmopolitan city,
Appreciating what life has blessed me with,
And ensuring that I make a mental note of this quiet city,
For I will never see it again in my life time.

The mountains (the first ever poem I wrote)

The streams that flow
With the sounds of coursing waters
The birds that fly
Expressing the beauties of nature
And the freedom I wished I had.

The flowers that bloom
Producing and aroma I longed to smell
And the mountains that have a hidden beauty
That draws my very soul.
These are the things I long for when I am in the cities.

From a mountain top
I view the world and the cities far away
How happy I am to feel alone
No noisy vehicles
No pollution
No news of evil that surrounds the world
And least of all
No one who will hurt my feelings.

It is a day or two that I am in the mountains
And I thank God for creating such beauty
That helps me drain my frustrations and keeps me at peace.

Printed in Great Britain
by Amazon